Ways I've Known Water

poems by

Lisa Breger

Finishing Line Press
Georgetown, Kentucky

Ways I've Known Water

For Annie

ACKNOWLEDGMENTS

"Time Under a Bridge" appeared in *Hunger Mountain*
"Leash" appeared in *The Lavender Review*
"I Need a Poem" and "After the Nor'easter" appeared in *Presence: A Journal of Catholic Poetry*
"Wintered Over" appeared in *Parabola*

Publisher: Leah Huete de Maines
Editor: Christen Kincaid
Cover Art: Lisa Breger
Author Photo: Anne E. Parker
Cover Design: Elizabeth Maines McCleavy

Order online: www.finishinglinepress.com
also available on amazon.com

Author inquiries and mail orders:
Finishing Line Press
PO Box 1626
Georgetown, Kentucky 40324
USA

Contents

Whenever winds blow,
the butterfly finds a new place
on the willow tree.

Matsuo Basho
trans. Sam Hamill

Time Under a Bridge

I don't want to leave this world:
My friends are in it, and there's so much beauty.
Even beneath the pigeon-pocked bridge—

the simple steel and concrete off-ramp
seeped with run-off, tubercular,
that runs over roadways and part of the river that leads nowhere—

there's a park bench, a gathering of squirrels around a stale loaf of bread.
Who wouldn't spend time here?
Yesterday, along the Greenway under cloudless late January sky

a flurry of bluebirds sang in the branches.
Today, I follow blue hospital signs near Boylston
neighborhood of pressure cooker bombs and recall

survivor Heather Abbot as I take the elevator to the malignancy floor.
They amputated the leg to heal her body.
My blood cells abnormally divide

that high-dose chemotherapies
target and destroy.
She painted the toenails on her prosthetic leg.

I shut my eyes and see the harbor:
gulls squawk over fishing boats along the docks,
dive for entrails, fish heads, and carry them triumphant through ocean air.

A Wish

How is it possible
  when not a cloud remains in the sky
    to drop to the bottom of the well?

How does it happen in this skin
  that covers muscle
    that covers bone

that shelters marrow?
  Trillions of hard working cells
    defend against disruption in life's busy house.

Is there an algorithmic sequence that = devolution
  and how many times does the sequence appear
    in which I carry on to myself about myself?

What might I want before I blow the candles out?
  Look at it this way,
    I could have missed the red fox cross our snow-covered yard.

The Downshift

I've become that old person I couldn't
stand driving behind when I was young.
The one who slows while maple leaves unfurl

on random Monday mornings in May.
Who stops at the crosswalk
to wave through the man with the cane.

I get it, I've run the light in my time
but now my eyes are bad
and there's pollen and I have no

place to go that's more important than overseeing
the safe passage of the giant snapping turtle
from one side of route number 9 to the next.

Oh go ahead and blow your horn, blow it again and speed off.
Can't you understand there's more than one red tail hawk
making an aerial arc above us

with the least bit of effort
tilting their wings
this way and that.

I know nothing else but miracles
after Walt Whitman

Morning dew on spring grass
sounds of children at play on Patriots day
and the Patriots come to life in reenactments
in Concord and Lexington, Charlestown and the North End.
Marathon runners, sinewy flesh and sweat

along the hilly route.
The water stations, the press cars, onlookers cheer
from behind barricades: the racers,
the winner's impressive times
and I remember the balloon man walking

back and forth at the base of heartbreak hill when I was young.
How I eyed the floating worlds
and my dad let me choose one wonder
the gruff man handing me the tender string I held all day.
Then it grew cold and only a few limping racers walked

among cups and orange peels
that littered the route
in grey light.
I took my last pass around the corner of Comm. Ave
to Washington and let the string go as I headed home; the blue

balloon lifted away on wind's wings
beyond telephone wires, tree peaks, church steeple
into empty sky and beyond
and what a miracle
to take a little piece of my heart and to fly.

Low Pressure Systems

Night so dark and hot the streets sizzle with steam
and thunder growls into peaks of heat lightening.
I was thinking of calling my brother who knows about weather
and may have been a meteorologist if it weren't for his bent

toward the kind of buck you make and lose at the racetrack.
A certain thrill of atmospheric changes traced down by satellite
or the way Don Kent could track a storm when we were kids.
My brother would tell me over again about Canada wind

slicing down to mix with the high-pressure system moving up the coast.
A love of danger or storm as if his whole paycheck was riding
on the seven-horse boxed in on the rail until the final stretch.
He's out of his seat, some thunder and lightning

hail the size of silver dollars, Nor'easter-no-school-announcements
charging down to the wire for a photo finish.
What's the payout, the odds lighting up the winner board
as he holds his fistful of tickets like an umbrella, his map of the sky.

Toothache

My smile hurt
    my head on the down pillow hurt

a pain behind the eye as if
    the throbbing world were a stop sign:

red, blinking, holding up traffic
    a jaw jammed shut.

When my mother calls, she asks
    upper right, says same as me

or from your father who, near the end,
    could never find his teeth

would flash a toothless smile at nurses
    for extra saltines, another cranberry juice.

One by one they disintegrate without fanfare
    or tooth-fairy visitations, just antibiotics

and astronomical dental bills that take months
    if not years to pay off.

A friend suggested travel to Costa Rica
    to save on the expense of it, another said Canada

but I'm already stitched up
    thinking of my father

behind the wheel of the old station wagon
    singing show tunes along the road to the World's fair

mother in the front seat, her teased and frosted hair
    bobbing above the headrest

as my brother & me fidget in the backseat
    candy kisses stuck to our teeth.

Morning, I sit

at the butcher-block table I use as a desk
a sturdy corpse, clutter-covered so its eyes
barely see itself in the mirror,
deforested, deaf

as silence that holds
a siren's cry through the night
and carries it like an oil spill
through the estuaries of my mind.

This table my first love stole from the open
mouth of a warehouse when it yawned in the pre-dusk,
knock-off hour and left her alone.
As I did, but kept the table

with its cigarette burn branded into the edge
when it was in our kitchen and held
a toaster oven, fruit bowl and portable TV.
It wasn't easy bringing it down the narrow stair case

that twisted from the 3rd to the 1st floor past the landlord's door.
But I had help, all these years, many hands
lift and carry what would be impossible
to shoulder alone.

Nervous System

Tick-tock clocks, clap on lights
Ring-camera doorbells are the tip of the iceberg.
There are those telemarketing calls, phishing emails
and the guy behind you at the red light that sits on his horn.
I just left a room with a wall clock and 3 small table tickers
and thought I'd lose my very in breath out breath mojo
that I've been learning from a Lama to calm.

You'd think my mind
wouldn't be a flea ridden dog.
But, what can you expect from a person who lived
her entire life with the sound of perpetual traffic?
Why didn't anyone send me to charm school, or teach me
to replace the look of terror with the obsequious smile?
If only I could figure out how to turn off Alexa's profanity filter.

Hey, it's not just me in the motel room
toweling over the smoke detector
to block its insensitive red eye that beams me into insomnia.
Don't you think the bat who can't echolocate
without pinging off rafters or going headlong
into the cell tower disguised as a pine
isn't plotting its survival with a roll of duct tape?

Just wait on hold with your cable company
or talk to an automated operator about payments
for a hospital bill triple the size of your mortgage
when all you wanted from your doctor was a quick look
at that thing growing on your neck
but instead—she turns to your emergency contact
—before she begins.

Cancer

It's not every day mortality
is a breakfast sandwich you pick up
to go, the crinkle wrap and a pepper packet
to tear open by the skin of your teeth.

After all, you're on your way to work
fingers fumble the strip of plastic lid you try to bend back
then—for no reason—the car in front
stops short and coffee spills on your quad.

Still, it's as ordinary as sitting at the red light in rush hour
all brake lights and backs of heads, and you think maybe
the light will change once or twice before you move an inch off the recliner
while the infusion of saline and unpronounceable chemicals completes.

Your spouse drives you home past where you used to work
and everything in sight moves with purpose and incomprehensible speed
at the bus stop at the intersection and along the pedestrian walkway
people with backpacks or with headsets are on important calls

while you, no longer capable of the driver's seat,
pink plastic pail between your legs, just want to linger longer in this life,
make it home to the dog who sniffs with no recognition
the strange smell that emanates from your pores.

You march back and forth to appointments in uniforms
that still have the outline of the soldier you used to be
your purple heart on your sleeve
as leaves fall from trees like little paratroopers

urging you on your own heroics:
to arrive on time, adoring your oncology nurse
whose job it is to insert the needle into your chest port
to administer the napalm bomb solution to cure cancer

but you worry what's happening or how you got here
and watch pieces of your former self, draft horse strength and suits of armor
casual acquaintances, family squabbles, professional responsibilities
ignite into a mushroom cloud and then settle on charred ground.

Days on end you watch out windows uplifted by the glory
of familiar oak trees, changeable skies, and three hawks
who circle the lake each day with your spirits underwing
while what's left of spring pushes up new shoots

the wild rabbits love you for.

Proof Positive

I believe in counting Mississippis
between thunder strikes
the source of courage to look up

and the credo *this too shall pass.*
I believe in the way the roof of our little yellow house
shines in moonlight and also the star beyond branches

of the mighty oak in the yard, the one next to the fish pond
I built with the two hands I believe in,
and the frogs that hop from the palms

of water lettuce spread along the surface.
It's the dog next to me breathing deeply
in and out that makes the sacred sound

as if love were a church bell
a bronze gong
going and gone…

What I Don't Know

Brownie's woman, her name, what she buried
in the yard: plate shard, nip bottle,
a push mower's wooden handle beneath the canopy of lilac.

In this house made of wood scraps from his construction jobs
a door sealed shut in a hallway
and where it leads, what of these light switches?

By my nightstand, pen inside pen-case
and beneath the velvet holder, crumbled words
of an old fortune, all it predicts.

A crawl space beyond the tornado shelter in a Kansas monastery
the lightning storm at night and what can be heard
through the window above the parlor door when all's still.

Who else saw thorns saw dark seeds open as flowers or bleeding hearts?
Did Elaine as she worked in silence to craft
a coffin for her monastic sister before digging her grave?

What is buried in me when I return
to the place I've never been:
flatlands by the bluffs

a low and dirty Missouri river;
What is carried on the current of prayer
and if there's wisdom in our wounds, that too?

Ode to Binoculars

When I lift you from the window ledge
and clock my eye sockets blur my vision
it takes time to get you right

like a lover who can't commit
and because of the dizzy way you make me feel
the whole grey world loses focus.

Remember how my father taught me to hold you and adjust the thumbwheel
when we sat in the racetrack grandstand
beneath clouds of cigar smoke and a wave of moths under stadium lights?

When he looked through you,
to the mare's bit and sweaty sheen, the jockey's whip,
we were on the edge of our bleacher seats

gambling away the future
but he held you steady as you delivered the fine print
cased in your dark shell.

And now, though morning aligns, old summer nights linger,
and you're heavy in my hands blocking out everything
except the blue jay's black eye staring down an empty feeder.

History Lesson

According to family lore, birds bring bad luck, the kind
my grandfather brought as a boy when he arrived at Ellis Island
sent in search of safer shores; his hands worked coarse

fabrics of a history he barely spoke of
and if you asked about migration
he'd look away as if perched on a far branch

a nest of silence assembled in the eaves of his chest,
those birds inside he tried to hide and whiskey away
until, from a coronary artery, one flew, and then another,

and we stood beneath blue
October sky and circling sparrows
that he'd watch from his wingback chair,

quiet as a mountain; and through the darkness I inherited
a large recurrent bird outside my window
a barred owl looking down on that part of my childhood

I spent with my grandfather at gaming halls and racetracks
the smoke-filled grandstands and lost wages
how the peanut man by the fountain attracted us to his pushcart

and we cracked shells and scattered kernels for pigeons closing in.
Could I go back, find some golden feather
or the way I was held under a grandmother's wing?

No birds she'd command as they called outside the window.
It was too late. There never was a window to the past
my grandfather spoke of, even though I carry its weight.

Even though my grandmother taught me to speak up in this world.
But no matter how outspoken, my words were never heard
unless they came out of a man's mouth
unless I towered over them and called them my own.

Grandmothers

They were from the days when a well-set table,
like a mother in pearls,
was admired down to the last glint of the salt spoon
in a country they never spoke of by name.
The old country, where their parents sang as they prayed
and sobbed as they left with silver wrapped in dishtowels.
Meals stewed on kitchen stoves,
brisket and potatoes,

rich as nobody's business, could only be settled with seltzer.
No meat with milk.
The kitchen was the workshop of these women grinding
special cuts in the hand grinder
chopping fried liver and onions with one boiled egg in a wooden bowl.
Chicken simmered with carrots, celery, parsnips—
strong soup to cure cold or chill from the child
or the stranger the child was told not to talk to, told
blood is thicker than gravy.

Set your place among these women
whose wrinkled hands were arthritic and thick
as a good suit bought in New York for an afternoon like this
to visit a neighbor's neighbor who made it big
in the garment business;
these women who sewed, these women who seldom drove—
they owned linen table clothes and good dishes and cologne
played canasta in Miami Beach and were married to heavy drinkers

who sold textiles on the road; women
who laughed at their husband's jokes but kept extra money
hidden among their girdles;
they believed in aspirin and peppermints
saved safety pins & rubber bands in old kitchen tins,
and, wearing floral house dresses,
kneaded and rolled out dough on floured counter tops—
women who faithfully made from scratch.

The morning of

I walked out to the pine point by the lake's edge
and scattered my thoughts like ashes along loose rock

the beach silt by the shallows.
The dog ran circles after darting swallows

whose iridescent wings caught glints of sun off cool water
and above us I remember an endless blue river of sky

as morning rush hour rumbled along the far-reaching highway
and between there and here, in the middle distance,

the muscular wings of a swan pair, their long caw, so mighty
as they crossed the lake's body in their stunning silver suits.

The world's arms were that open which is how I knew it was time:
time to take it all with me, and time to leave it all behind.

Hardly

All's quiet and blue this cold winter morning
the dog asleep in the upholstered chair.

Outside beneath the feeder two squirrels feast on fallen seed.
Inside I read the surrealist's book of poems *Shock by Shock*

the first since his second heart and use the word transplant
to describe my own ordeal though it was hardly

a transplant— some blood out, some blood in
and if it weren't for the orange lunch box they shuttled the cells off in

one wouldn't have an inkling.
But here I am in the dead of winter listening to the hum of the monitor

I mistake for the kind of silence a crow interrupts—
the bird as large as the plate glass window another bird flies into:

So much for hope being that thing with wings, unless you count
the helicopter that medevacs the organ edited into the poet's chest.

Maybe I was a forest on the brink of unsustainability,
the controlled burn my best option for survival

so long as transplanted cells grow in the marrow.
A dabble in the afterlife and who knows whose heart beats on.

Fall, after all

Technically they were sick days
but imagine the semester begins, Indian summer
and you're still futzing around in short sleeves

having coffee on the patio as the sun glistens over the lake
where you'll walk the dog later and go for a swim
because the water's still summer-warm

and you're not in rush hour worrying
you left the morning handouts
on the dining room table and will have to wing it

in front of the new batch of students who already dislike you
grumble about your syllabus of relentless assignments
but it's past add/drop so they're stuck with you, relieved you messed up

or are out sick given the way you walk around the room
call on random people so they have to half listen
which requires more effort than they're willing to give, even though

you spent your whole summer preparing *compelling* coursework
yet when the clock nears the hour that class ends
they've already packed up their backpacks and put on coats

and even as you quote Shakespeare as if conducting a symphony
you've lost them and they file out while you call after them
don't forget the reading see you Thursday have a nice day.

They'll come back Thursday to complain they didn't get the assignment
to the teacher in your place who created his own syllabus
as you butter a second scone add a touch of jam

a neighbor made and brought to cheer you
because you had your first chemo treatment
and now there's a certain spring in your step

the kind you have on vacation
as you head to the lake with your dog and your beach chair
and don't have to learn a single student name

or give feedback on their work and figure out grades
only the medicinal taste that feels a bit like burnt toast and tin cans
and tingles down to the toes which are in the water's edge—

Ah this is the life you think as you look up
from the new novel your friend wrote
I could get used to this.

I Need a Poem

to wrap its arms around my tired shoulders and pull me close,
a poem that knows I've been up all night coughing, the medicine
burning and on my many trips in the dark to the bathroom
knows I tracked the flight status of my spouse's plane over Saudi Arabia
and let the dog out again under piercing stars.

A poem that interrupts incoming text messages
with the pronouncement I'm without answers
here alone, the Kleenex box by my side
and a work schedule ticking
as anxiously as the Sunday *60 Minutes* clock.

I need a poem like a deep breath, a poem
that makes a good stew from roots and bones
one the dog didn't bury behind the shed
beneath leaves and stones, one that suggests itself
upward like spring shoots

but less fleeting by which I mean the trellis
by the dogwood that holds pruned branches of the rosebush up.
A poem that not only brings soup
but sits for a spell, butters warm bread
and feeds us as sun lowers itself brilliantly beyond the horizon

Autumn Embrace

Golden beech leaves scattered along a dry pine path
late summer's last mile

where we make our way, the old dog careful over tree roots and fallen acorns
paths she used to run.
She stops to smell a fallen branch or bit of browning brush,

looks back toward me, as the lake
darkens and through the greying fields of sky
the Canada geese call out for home.

If this is the last of it, let me hold on
as the bumblebee on late blooming phlox
let me feel sun on my face as she paints the maple crowns with gold.

I pull the boats for the season, bring the house plants
inside by the picture window and admire their leafy growth.

Soon the sound of rake tines and gathering
the last of the blackberries,
crisp, tart apples and baking pies.

Later, in the owl dark dawn of early October
I crack the window just a bit, then a bit more.
The years it took to open to my life;
Harvest hidden Concord grapes
that grow wild and heavy on their vines.

The Work

The patience to listen for words that take their time
maturing from whines groans whispers to a finer
wisdom that can be shared like bread
broken and gifted;

The stamina to sit with the difficult
the runaway, the wounded and anxious
to not only look but intimately
sequence the heartbeats

the marrow of the matter.
How easy to drift from the source, pulled by the current
of Tuesdays to-do list to get milk, call the plumber, answer email.
Is it so important, more so say than the altar

the everyday invitations outside the window.
The owl in the evergreen peak
or robins eating winterberries.
Why drink from an empty cup?

The thirst is for gardener's work, to kneel
as one does before the word
the word being the world
the dark earth and all that shines

notes of wild onion in air the spring fed
the mountain knowledge old wisdom of oaks
fluttering feet of the field mouse in the office wall
the disrepair of silence in which everything sings.

Elegy in Snow
for my father

Hungry geese flock to feed on snow covered fields,
and spread like a dark cloud
as ice along the river breaks below the surface
and makes a mournful sound.
How many winters, how many walks

have I walked this snow-hardened path
where sometimes I sink in, fall hard and have to pull myself up
the way you showed me the jab, the hook,
how to keep punching through chemo,
contusion on your forehead from your last fall

skin bruised beneath my bandage.
How many days as shockingly clear
as the day snowmelt made its way across the bend in the trail
and I trudged under the sun's glare
to cross precisely here

precisely where I took the call
that you were gone,
not anywhere in particular that I could imagine,
weightless,
blue winter air.

Could you know the trees
how startled they stood
how frozen the icy ground
how far afield I found myself?
My first fatherless steps

as uncertain as toddling toward you
in an old home movie,
a grainy black and white.
Figures in snowsuits wave to the camera
their mouths mouthing inaudible words.

Deeper in December, outside the picture window,
sheets of snow drift as they did during the blizzard of 78
and obscure my view with white shrouds of frozen mist
the way death distances how I know you—
no call about road conditions

or talk of the great storms we shoveled through
my sullen teenage years,
no talk of sports or games we watched, our religion,
the plays you taught me to believe in
for the game-ender, the buzzer beater

how to get open down field for the Hail Mary—
no guts, no glory you'd say.
The bones of the house shiver.
You are far away and closer than ever
a blank page, an absence of words.

Urn

I take pieces of my father for open air rides and Sunday drives
west on 117 as if there's enough of him to admire

the way the road winds over the Assabet River
like the bridge that went up over our differences,

unspoken as they remained, though sometimes
I feel shaped by the absence of his words as if

inside the mind's drawers there's an empty chest
nothing to fill in the blanks those years he couldn't look at me.

Just drive, he'd say wanting none of this
and leaning back in the passenger's side

glad not to be behind the wheel of responsibility
and maybe it was only one ride on Father's Day

that I took him down from the shelf
palm sized, bottled up

as the time my mother made him visit me
and we played pool in silence but before he left he said

I'm still your father you know
but it was never like before.

Before we used to take long rides and sing along with the radio
sing loud and spirited as if we both were good.

After the Nor'easter

Every aftermath glistens:
the boxer up off the mat at the bout's end
the cracked windshield a mosaic
the patient in recovery with a morphine glow.

Even the large limb torn from the great oak
that hangs against the powerline has a last gasper's brilliance
though our lights been knocked out for days
and the tree's prognosis questionable

which is how we live now
weak-kneed in the aftermath.
The fever breaks and heart backpedals to cruising speed
the house aglow in candlelight.

Soon daybreak appears in lavender and sequins
and we're all big-eyed at the picture window
ready to dance with our discharge papers
fall over backwards and make angels in the snow.

Courtyard

Magnolia blossoms float like sailboats in the wind
and I sit in the hospital courtyard under blue sky on a sunny day
a year after construction of the school building across Brookline Ave

where I watched from my hospital window
the harnessed steel workers in their orange vests and hard hats
guide crane-held beams in place as they bounced along the building's bones.

I was there for a few stories,
and when night came on and the crane stood silent,
the emptiness was a hallway I'd walk down in a blue gown

dragging an iv pole through artificial light.
Now the finished building
glistens in the sun by the playing field and I'm no longer behind glass

staring out at soundless city lights and bruised night sky,
my breathing drowned out by the sound of monitors and machines.
I look back at myself hooked up in the bone marrow transplant room

and imagine the person there now
all those on the oncology floor
the protracted days and strange nights

when life felt so far away.
Yet today how happily the magnolia blossoms fall
and cover the patio with their beautiful confetti.

Wintered Over

Water carries sunlight along a narrow twisting stream;
      sunlight glitters on the water's back
         light among dark trees.
            I watch a hawk in the distance glide the thermals

rise and circle the open space over Lake Cochituate.
      Soon it will be lilac season
         among other kindnesses.
            To have weathered this harsh winter

didn't take courage or strength
      though the lilacs are hardy
         and the season brings forth.
            How can I have nothing to say about this;

a survivor always has a story.
      Maybe you just keep on living
         even when the odds are against you.
            A nurse brings a saucer of milk to your lips

and the cat in you,
      how many lives now,
         takes a swallow.
            Then, you lift a hand and take her hand,

another sip,
      and lift yourself up
         which is what I remember.
            Transplanted stem cells find their way back to the marrow.

I was neither strong nor brave.
      I stayed in bed and looked out the window.
         Some days the old oaks across the way swayed in the wind
            other days: stillness and birds.

I don't know why I made it.
      Don't we all have a fierce desire
         to see a hummingbird
            drink from the trumpet vine?

Ways I've Known Water

The pond froze in winter and the sound of skates along ice
until spring thaw brought peepers and high water
that ran over rock-beds forming streams behind houses
and in summer the dry stone made an easy crossover
and when they dredged the pond the perch laid flat in mud,

some I rescued and rehomed,
some lived until they refilled,
and there I followed the streams far from home
or spent lucky summers at beaches diving in waves
or digging in sand or finding shells and sea glass along the shoreline

and explored waterways along the southern coast
side-armed flat stones along bodies of water
to see how many skips a toss would take
and watched the ripples expand
and got caught in downpours that swept away

street debris down roadway streams that emptied into catch basins
where I watched the rush of water, sticks, leaves, road grit
enter lakes and rivers and fill into oceans and navigated
the locks in small boats with little direction and stood in spring rain
for the softness on my face or worked in rain

that washed sweat from my brow on hot summer days
and watered gardens from rain barrels or lake water
submerging my bucket beneath the surface and listened
to the gurgling of it filling and lugging it up in the swoosh
and walking wet pavements and drinking from fountains

and finding a source in drought or day zero's iv fluids
damp cloths to the forehead.
Returned to the sound of water of waves breaking against rock
the churning sea dragging sand back into itself,
waves I rode or was pulled out by currents and beached along sandbars

or pranced in puddles, making a splash or listening to rain
on the roof on leaves and droplets down windows
the swish of wipers on windshields
the splash as the car hit puddles and slowed
or fish in the road when the river ran its banks

and stretched wide arms as if waking from fitful sleep
to thrash and rush over fields filling wetlands
rearranging the landscape the way ocean storms
tore through sea walls swallowed homes and roads
the many storms I rode out

that took the lives of loved ones more deserving
to stand here on the banks and speak of it.

Lisa Breger is an award-winning poet, educator, and canine massage therapist. She teaches poetry as a spiritual practice in many settings across the country including the Benet House Retreat Center for the Sisters of St. Benedict at St. Mary Monastery in Rock Island, Illinois. She is also the founder of the Wayland Poetry Garden, a community arts project funded by the Wayland Cultural Council. She has won many awards including the Grolier Poetry Prize, The Thomas Merton Award for Poetry of the Sacred, and was a runner-up for the Ruth Stone Poetry Prize. Currently, her poems appear in *Presence: A Journal of Catholic Poetry, Parabola, Hunger Mountain, The Lavender Review*, and the anthology *Love is for All of Us: Poems of Tenderness and Belonging* edited by Brad Peacock and James Crews.

9798899902819